The Crisp Approach to

WORDPERFECT
styles made easy

by Geraldine Mosher

The *Crisp Computer* Series

Editor: David Foster
Project Manager: David Foster
Interior Design: Kathleen Gadway
Cover Design: Kathleen Gadway

Library of Congress No 93-70782

ISBN 1-56052-217-8

WordPerfect is the registered trademark of WordPerfect Corporation.

Crisp Computer Book Series

These books are not like other books. Inspired by the widely successful "Fifty-Minute" Crisp Books, these books provide the least you need to know in order to use today's most popular application software packages. Specifically designed for either self-study or business training, they are "the fifty-minute books that teach!"

These guides are not for technical wizards or power users. They are for the average business person who is not familiar with computers nor comfortable with a particular software package—such as WordPerfect, Lotus 1-2-3, or Excel.

In most everyday computer applications, employees, managers, and students do not need to learn every feature and capability of their software. What most business users want is simply the amount of knowledge—delivered as quickly and painlessly as possible—to perform specific duties: write the letter, report or newsletter; create the budget or sales forecast; set up a mailing list; and other important business tasks. These books use everyday business examples to guide readers step-by-step through just those commands that they will use most.

Concise and practical, the Crisp fifty-minute computer books provide quick, easy ways to learn today's most popular computer software applications.

Other Books in the
Crisp Computer Series

Contents

1

Introduction to WordPerfect's Styles

What Is a Style?

WordPerfect's style feature is a powerful tool for formatting documents. It allows complex combinations of formatting codes to be inserted in text with just a few keystrokes. Text and graphics can also be entered into a document with a style. Although you can do the same things with macros, there are substantial differences between macros and styles. The most useful aspect of styles becomes obvious when you need to make a formatting change.

Styles allow you to make sure that all the elements of a document are uniform and allow you to maintain consistency between documents. They also allow you to quickly change the design and layout of your document when needed.

Creating a style involves entering formatting codes, text, graphics, or any combination of these elements into a style definition. This saves you from entering all the formatting codes manually each time you want to format a piece of text a certain way.

When you use a style, WordPerfect inserts a single code that contains all of the formatting, text, and graphics that you have placed in the style. When WordPerfect encounters a style code in a document, it checks to see the current contents of the style. Therefore, if you change a style, WordPerfect updates every occurrence of the style automatically.

Who Uses Styles?

- Office workers
    (to prepare a wide variety of documents)

- Presenters
    (to produce transparencies)

- Students
    (to format term papers and theses)

- Authors
    (to prepare manuscripts)

- Publishers
    (to format newsletters)

- Anyone who wants
    · to speed up the formatting process

    · to maintain formatting consistency

    · to simplify formatting revision

Why Use Styles?

To provide consistent formatting within a document: A document will not create a good impression if one subheading is in bold type at the left margin and another is underlined in the center, or if one title is in large type and another in very large. Using styles allows you to consistently replicate a particular format throughout the document.

To provide consistent formatting for similar documents: A person or a group can set up standards for items such as annual reports, memos, letters, and policy statements, and be sure that everyone is following the correct format. If there is a decision to change the format, only the styles need be changed—not the individual documents.

To reduce code clutter: Using styles decreases the amount of codes, particularly at the beginning of the document. Using a style to format an entire document inserts only one code at the beginning of the document. This avoids the jumble of codes that would normally be there when a number of format codes are needed. This also prevents the cursor from getting in between the initial codes by mistake and causing problems.

For ease of revision: The styles feature provides an easy way to change formats. Imagine that you typed all the section titles of a manual using large type and now you wanted to change these to very large type. To change each one individually would be very time consuming, particularly because you cannot use *Replace* (**Alt-F2**) to substitute most formatting codes. But a simple change of the style codes changes each occurrence of that style instantly!

To automate the process of formatting: Using styles to format an entire document not only ensures that the formatting will be consistent regardless of who types the document, but it also automates the process—formatting becomes faster, easier, and more dependable.

Differences Between Styles and Macros

Many people feel that a macro can do whatever a style can do, so there is no reason to learn another feature that does the same thing. While macros are powerful and easy to use, styles have one big advantage over macros (or entering codes manually): you can easily change something you have done repeatedly. If you have ever changed your mind, you should learn to use styles.

A document looks the same whether you enter the text, graphics, and formatting codes manually, by macro, or by style. But the codes are not identical. Manually entered codes and codes inserted by a macro appear the same; style codes are different. When you use a style, only the style codes appear, not the individual formatting codes that make up the style.

Editing is easier with styles than with macros. Manually entered codes and codes inserted by a macro must be changed one at a time; style codes are changed within the style (once) and affect all occurrences. For example, if you used a macro to insert formatting codes in twenty places to format some element of a document and later wanted to change those codes, you would need to make the change twenty times. If you used a style twenty times in a document, editing the style once would automatically change all twenty occurrences of the formatting.

Differences Between WordPerfect 5.0 and 5.1

- The style feature introduced in WordPerfect 5.0 had only two types of styles (open and paired). WordPerfect 5.1 added a third type (outline).
- WordPerfect 5.1 increased the options for deleting styles from a style library. A style library is a file that contains a number of styles. There are now three deletion choices: (1) delete the style and convert the codes contained in the style into regular codes wherever the style was used, (2) delete the style entirely including the codes, and (3) delete the style definition only. Deleting a style in WordPerfect 5.0 is the same as using Delete Style (Definition Only) in WordPerfect 5.1.
- WordPerfect 5.0 did not allow you to use graphics in styles. In WordPerfect 5.1 graphics can be put into styles utilizing the "Graphics on Disk" option.
- The ready-made styles (LIBRARY.STY) included in WordPerfect 5.0 and 5.1 are different. WordPerfect 5.0 included only four paired styles. WordPerfect 5.1 includes two paired, three outline, and two open styles.

Lesson 1 Summary

What is a style?

A style is a feature that allows you to insert formatting codes, text, and graphics into a document with ease and consistency.

Who uses styles?

Anyone who wants

- to speed up the process of formatting
- to maintain consistency in formatting
- to make revising formats easier

Why are styles used?

Styles are used

- to provide consistent formatting within a document
- to provide consistent formatting for similar documents
- to reduce code clutter, for ease of revision
- to automate the process of formatting

Differences between styles and macros

Codes inserted with macros are just the same as manually inserted codes; style codes are different, but affect the document in the same way. Editing is easier with styles than with macros because editing the style automatically changes all occurrences of that style. Codes entered with a macro must be changed individually

Differences between WordPerfect 5.0 and 5.1

WordPerfect 5.1

- added outline styles
- increased deletion options
- added graphics capability
- provided more ready-made styles

Notes

_____

_____

_____

_____

_____

_____

_____

_____

_____

_____

_____

_____

_____

_____

_____

_____

_____

_____

_____

_____

_____

_____

_____

_____

_____

Notes

_____

_____

_____

_____

_____

_____

_____

_____

_____

_____

_____

_____

_____

_____

_____

_____

_____

_____

_____

_____

_____

_____

_____

LESSON

2

Types of Styles

Determining the Style Type

The following lessons explain how to create and use open styles, paired styles, and outline styles. Before you begin to create a style, however, you need to know which of the three types of styles you want to create.

How do you decide which type to use? To make the right choice, you need to understand the basic properties of each style. The remainder of this lesson will describe the three types of styles and give examples of how and where you might use each type.

Outline Styles

- Outline styles are used for any material that needs to be arranged in levels.
- The Paragraph Number Definition menu [*Outline* (**Shift-F5**), **D**efine (6)] that is used to choose outline formats contains only simple outline formats. If you want to add any features to the outline, you need to use an outline style. Using an outline style, you can create customized styles for up to eight levels of an outline.
- An outline style can be defined in either the paragraph numbering menu or the style menu but can be used only through the paragraph numbering menu. Once you select an outline style, that style is used to number paragraphs and create outlines.

Open Styles

- An open style is applied to a document at the location of the cursor.
- Open styles remain in effect until the end of the document or until another code changes some part of the format.
- Open codes (tab sets, margins, justification, etc.) are usually placed into open styles.
- If you want to include text and graphics in a style, they are usually put into an open style.
- Open styles are usually used to format an entire document.

Paired Styles

- A paired style takes effect at the location of the cursor and remains in effect until it is turned off.
- A paired style is turned on at the beginning of a segment of text and turned off at the end. The style affects only the text between the "ON" and "OFF" codes.
- Paired codes (italics, underline, bold) are usually placed in paired styles.
- Paired styles are frequently used to format titles, chapter headings, and subheadings.

Examples of Style Types

Let's take a look at some specific uses for styles. This will help you determine the type of style you want to create.

Letterheads

Open: Use to do overall formatting and to insert the text, graphic lines, and graphic boxes desired for the letterhead.

Setting up different letterhead styles allows you to choose the letterhead you want: formal or informal, fancy or plain, striking or subdued. Choose a letterhead according to the impression you wish to make. The letterhead styles can include not only the formatting necessary for the letter, but can also include a logo, graphic lines, and graphic boxes.

Envelopes

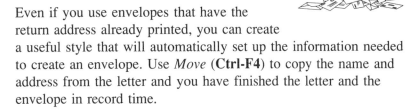

Open: Use to set up the necessary formatting. Include the return address, if desired.

Even if you use envelopes that have the return address already printed, you can create a useful style that will automatically set up the information needed to create an envelope. Use *Move* (**Ctrl-F4**) to copy the name and address from the letter and you have finished the letter and the envelope in record time.

Term Papers and Theses

Open: Use for overall formatting, one for each instructor or type of document, if necessary.

Paired: Use for quotations, chapter or section titles, subheadings. Include markings for the Table of Contents.

Outline: Use to have the outline feature automatically indent after each level.

Imagine a college student who needs to submit a number of term papers. Each professor has different requirements—particular margins, spacing, type size, and so on. Using open styles simplifies the task. Once the styles are set up, simply choose the desired style from a list and instantly the term paper is properly formatted for that particular class.

Paired styles are used for long quotations. Even though the rest of the paper is double spaced, long quotations may need to be single spaced. In addition, long quotations may need to be in italics and double indented (indented from both the left and the right margins). All of this can be taken care of with a paired style. The main advantage to using the paired style is that when the style is turned off, all of the prior defaults are restored: the font, spacing, and other formatting elements are restored to what they were before the style.

Other paired styles for chapter titles, section headings and subheadings, and outlines help the student streamline formatting tasks.

Invoices

Open: Use for overall formatting of invoices including a heading with a graphic, if desired.

Paired: Use to set up column headings, tab sets, math definition and turn math on.

An open style assists the creation of an attractive invoice. However, using a paired style for the formatting necessary to use WordPerfect's math feature (tabs, math definition, etc.) will save considerable time.

Manuscripts

Open: Use for the overall formatting, one for each type of writing or for each publisher, as necessary.

Paired: Use for dialogue sections in scripts, chapter titles, quotations, and so on.

When submitting a manuscript to an editor, the formatting required varies depending on the type of manuscript (short story, magazine article, novel, etc.). Each form of fiction and non-fiction has its own format. Many books have been written detailing the correct format for submission of different types of manuscripts. Many editors and publishers will not accept manuscripts submitted in the wrong format. Styles are a boon to the freelance writer.

Newsletters

Open: Use for the overall formatting (including the column setup) and to insert the text and graphics for the masthead.

Paired: Use for article titles.

Creating a newsletter requires extensive formatting. Therefore, styles are absolutely essential for the preparation of newsletters. Create one open style for the overall formatting and the masthead and paired styles for the article titles.

Everything

Open: Use to set up formats for different kinds of documents.

Paired: Use for hanging paragraphs and bulleted lists.

Outline: Use to have the outline feature automatically indent after each level; use to have the level designators bolded, underlined or changed to a different font size; use if you need any specialized outline.

Because of the inherent properties of open styles (i.e., they take effect at the location of the cursor and stay on), the simplest and most common use of an open style is to format an entire document—any type of document. Although the codes can be entered manually, using styles does away with the clutter of codes at the beginning of the document, and helps avoid using an incorrect format (i.e., from the wrong professor). It also prevents "code splitting"—getting your cursor in the middle of the codes at the top of a document by mistake.

Lesson 2 Summary

Determining the Style Type

The type of style you create is determined by the properties of each type of style and by what the style will be used for.

Outline Styles

An outline style, used to arrange material hierarchically, is used with the paragraph numbering feature.

Open Styles

An open style, usually used to format an entire document, remains in effect until the end of the document or until changed.

Paired Styles

A paired style, used to format a section of text, is turned on and turned off.

Examples of Style Types

Use open styles for letterheads and envelopes. Use open and paired styles for invoices, manuscripts, and newsletters. Term papers and theses use open, paired, and outline styles. Many other documents can also use all three types of styles.

Notes

Notes

_____

_____

_____

_____

_____

_____

_____

_____

_____

_____

_____

_____

_____

_____

_____

_____

_____

_____

_____

_____

_____

_____

_____

_____

3

Creating Styles

Creating a style involves naming and defining a style, and specifying what format codes, text, or graphics will go into the style.

Before starting to create or use styles, you may want to check your setup to see where WordPerfect will be saving the styles. See "Checking the Present Style Setup" in Lesson 5. Because styles are saved differently than documents, you may also want to read the information on how styles are saved in Lesson 5.

How to Create an Open Style

1. Press *Style* (**Alt-F8**)

   The Style List screen appears. Your screen should look like one of the two following screens:

Figure 3.1
Empty Style List screen

```
Styles

  Name      Type    Description





  1 On; 2 Off; 3 Create; 4 Edit; 5 Delete; 6 Save; 7 Retrieve; 8 Update: 1
```

WordPerfect Styles Made Easy

Figure 3.2
Style List screen with
LIBRARY.STY

```
Styles

Name        Type      Description

Bibliogrphy Paired    Bibliography
Doc Init    Paired    Initialize Document Style
Document    Outline   Document Style
Pleading    Open      Header for numbered pleading paper
Right Par   Outline   Right-Aligned Paragraph Numbers
Tech Init   Open      Initialize Technical Style
Technical   Outline   Technical Document Style



1 On; 2 Off; 3 Create; 4 Edit; 5 Delete; 6 Save; 7 Retrieve; 8 Update: 1
```

If the list is empty (first screen), continue with Step 2. If the list is not empty (second screen), you are looking at a list of styles in a style library. You will first need to delete the listed styles. Deleting the styles from this list only deletes them from the current document; it does not delete them permanently.

To delete the styles from the list:

• Highlight a style name
• Press **D**elete (5)
• Press **D**efinition Only (3)

Repeat these three steps until the list is empty.

For more information on style libraries, see Lesson 5, "Saving Styles." For more information on deleting styles, see Lesson 6, "Other Operations."

18

2. Choose **C**reate (3)

The Style Edit screen appears:

```
┌─────────────────────────────────────────────┐
│  Styles: Edit                                 │
│                                               │
│     1 - Name                                  │
│                                               │
│     2 - Type            Paired                │
│                                               │
│     3 - Description                           │
│                                               │
│     4 - Codes                                 │
│                                               │
│     5 - Enter           HRt                   │
│                                               │
│                                               │
│  Selection: 0                                 │
└─────────────────────────────────────────────┘
```

3. Choose **T**ype (2)

The following menu appears at the bottom of the screen:

Type: **1 P**aired; **2 O**pen; **3** Outline: **0**

4. Choose **O**pen (2)

Notice that "5 - Enter" disappeared from the screen. That selection is not needed for open styles.

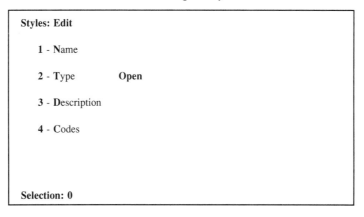

```
┌─────────────────────────────────────────────┐
│  Styles: Edit                                 │
│                                               │
│     1 - Name                                  │
│                                               │
│     2 - Type            Open                  │
│                                               │
│     3 - Description                           │
│                                               │
│     4 - Codes                                 │
│                                               │
│                                               │
│                                               │
│  Selection: 0                                 │
└─────────────────────────────────────────────┘
```

5. Choose **N**ame (1)

The cursor moves past "1 - Name." If you don't give the style a name, WordPerfect will give it a number.

6. Type a style name and press **Enter**

 A style name can have up to 12 characters, including spaces.

7. Choose **D**escription (3)

 The cursor moves past "3 - Description."

8. Type a description and press **Enter**

 The description can have up to 54 characters, including spaces. The description should contain either an indication of the contents of the style or how the style will be used. It is also a good practice to include the current date as a part of the description. If the style is changed later, remember to change the date included in the description. A good description helps to identify the style.

9. Choose **C**odes (4)

 You will see a split screen.

Figure 3.5
Style Codes screen (open style)

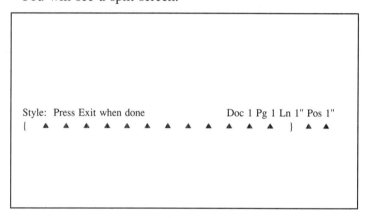

Style: Press Exit when done   Doc 1 Pg 1 Ln 1" Pos 1"

The split screen is similar to a regular document screen with reveal codes on. The top part shows how the document appears on your normal document screen—the codes do not show but their results do. The bottom part shows the text and codes just as a reveal codes screen would.

10. Insert the codes

 Enter any codes or text that you want in the style. Enter the codes the same way you would enter them if you were in the regular document screen. See "Notes on Open Style Codes" below.

11. Press *Exit* (**F7**) three times

    The first *Exit* returns you to the Style Edit screen.

    The second *Exit* returns you to the Style List screen.

    The third *Exit* returns you to your document.

NOTE

NOTE: Do not clear your screen at this point or you will lose the style that you created. You must save either the document or the style. For more information see Lesson 5, "Saving Styles."

Notes on Open Style Codes

- Open styles stay in effect throughout the document or until WordPerfect encounters another code that changes the format. For example, if an open style contains a code for a 1.5" left margin, that margin stays in effect for the entire document. However, if on page 3 of the document there is a manually entered code for a 2" left margin, the 2" code overrides the 1.5" code and the left margin from that point on will be 2".

- When including codes in a style, it is a good idea to put in codes even for some default settings. For example, you may want to enter a code for single spacing in case the spacing before the style was changed from the default. If you enter the default codes, you are sure to get exactly what you want.

- Graphics that are used in styles are not stored in the document. They are stored on disk. When you put graphics into styles, WordPerfect automatically selects "Graphic On Disk" and puts it in the Contents option. The actual figure is not placed in the style, only the filename of the graphic.

- Don't use a date in a style. *Date Text* (**Shift-F5**, **2**) will show the date the style was created and will never change. *Date Code* (**Shift-F5**, **1**) will change every time you retrieve or print the document. It would be best to create a macro that selects the style and then inserts the date.

- Although styles can contain text, graphics, and formatting codes, they cannot contain keystrokes for functions or actions (exiting, running the speller or thesaurus, running a macro, etc.).

- Also, there are some features that cannot be placed directly into a style (paragraph number definition, table of contents definition). However, it is possible to use *Move* (**Ctrl-F4**) to move these codes from the document screen to the styles codes screen. In this way, the codes are entered into the style.

How to Create a Paired Style

1. Press *Style* (**Alt-F8**)

   The Style List screen appears. Your screen should look like one of the two following screens:

Figure 3.6
Empty Style List screen

```
┌─────────────────────────────────────────────────────────┐
│  Styles                                                   │
│                                                           │
│    Name       Type    Description                         │
│                                                           │
│                                                           │
│                                                           │
│                                                           │
│                                                           │
│                                                           │
│                                                           │
│                                                           │
│                                                           │
│  1 On; 2 Off; 3 Create; 4 Edit; 5 Delete; 6 Save; 7 Retrieve; 8 Update: 1 │
└─────────────────────────────────────────────────────────┘
```

Figure 3.7
*Style List screen with
LIBRARY.STY*

```
┌─────────────────────────────────────────────────────────┐
│  Styles                                                   │
│                                                           │
│    Name       Type    Description                         │
│                                                           │
│    Bibliogrphy Paired  Bibliography                       │
│    Doc Init    Paired  Initialize Document Style          │
│    Document    Outline Document Style                     │
│    Pleading    Open    Header for numbered pleading paper │
│    Right Par   Outline Right-Aligned Paragraph Numbers    │
│    Tech Init   Open    Initialize Technical Style         │
│    Technical   Outline Technical Document Style           │
│                                                           │
│                                                           │
│  1 On; 2 Off; 3 Create; 4 Edit; 5 Delete; 6 Save; 7 Retrieve; 8 Update: 1 │
└─────────────────────────────────────────────────────────┘
```

If the list is empty (first screen), continue with Step 2. If the list is not empty (second screen), you are looking at a list of styles in a style library. You will need to delete the listed styles. Deleting styles from this list only deletes them from the current document; it does not delete them permanently.

To delete the styles from the list:

- Highlight a style name
- Press **D**elete (5)
- Press **D**efinition Only (3)

Repeat these three steps until the list is empty.

For more information on style libraries, see Lesson 5, "Saving Styles." For more information on deleting styles, see Lesson 6, "Other Operations."

2. Choose **C**reate (3)

The Style Edit screen appears:

Figure 3.8
Empty Style Edit screen

```
Styles: Edit

    1 - Name

    2 - Type          Paired

    3 - Description

    4 - Codes

    5 - Enter         HRt


Selection: 0
```

The default type is Paired. You do not need to change the type.

3. Choose **N**ame (1)

The cursor moves past "1 - Name." If you don't give the style a name, WordPerfect will give it a number.

4. Type a style name and press **Enter**

A style name can have up to 12 characters, including spaces.

5. Choose **D**escription (3)

The cursor moves past "3 - Description."

6. Type a description and press **Enter**

The description can have up to 54 characters, including spaces. The description should contain either an indication of the contents of the style or how the style will be used. It is also a good practice to include the current date as a part of the description. If the style is changed later, remember to change the date included in the description. A good description helps to identify the style.

7. Choose **E**nter (5)

The following menu appears across the bottom of the screen:

Enter: **1** HRt; **2** Off; **3** Off/On: **0**

8. Choose 1, 2, or 3

When you create a paired style, you need to choose how the **Enter** key will operate. You can designate one of the following:

HRt (1): The **Enter** key acts exactly as it normally does. Use **H**Rt when the style affects text that extends over paragraphs or consists of multiple lines (i.e., the style will be applied to text that contains HRt's so you want the **Enter** key to behave normally).

O**ff** (2): The **Enter** key will move the cursor past the off code, thereby turning the style off. Use O**ff** when the style will affect only one paragraph or only one line, as in a title.

Off/**O**n (3): The **Enter** key will turn the style off, then turn it back on again. Use Off/**O**n for a series of similar paragraphs or lines, consecutive hanging paragraphs, bulleted lists, multiple lines that need to be centered, etc.

9. Choose **C**odes (4)

You will see a split screen.

Figure 3.9
Style Codes screen (paired style)

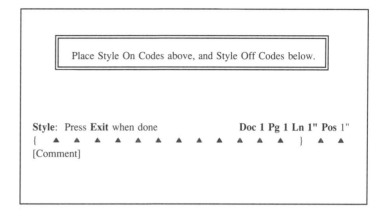

The split screen is similar to a regular document screen with reveal codes on. The top part shows how the document appears on your normal document screen—the codes do not show but their results do. The bottom part shows the text and codes just as a reveal codes screen would.

The box in the upper part of the screen that says "Place Style On Codes Above, and Style Off Codes Below" and the [Comment] code in the lower part of the screen both represent the text that the style will affect. If the cursor in the upper screen is above the box, then the cursor in the bottom screen is to the left of the [Comment] code. If the upper cursor is underneath the box, the lower cursor is to the right of the [Comment] code.

The [Comment] code is acting as a divider for the on and off codes. Codes that appear before the comment code are activated when the style is turned on, codes after the comment code are activated when the style is turned off. The [Comment] code and the code box above appear only for paired styles because they apply only to a particular block of text.

10. Insert the codes

    Enter any codes or text that you want in the style. Enter the codes the same way you would enter them if you were on the regular document screen. Enter all the codes you want to activate when the style is turned on. Then use the **Right Arrow** to pass the [Comment] box and enter all the codes you

25

want to activate when the style is turned off. See "Notes on Paired Style Codes" below.

11. Press *Exit* (**F7**) three times

   The first *Exit* returns you to the Style Edit screen.

   The second *Exit* returns you to the Style List screen.

   The third *Exit* returns you to your document.

NOTE

   NOTE: Do not clear your screen at this point or you will lose the style that you created. You must save either the document or the style. For more information see Lesson 5, "Saving Styles."

Notes on Paired Style Codes

- When creating a paired style, you enter any text, graphics, or codes you want activated when the style is turned on before the [Comment] code and put any codes you want activated when the style is turned off after the [Comment] code. However, you do not need to enter many "OFF" codes. It is not necessary to insert "OFF" codes for most formatting changes because WordPerfect automatically resets the format to whatever existed before the style was turned on. Codes in the "ON" section are reset when you turn off a style (except Format: Page codes) even if the code exists in the "OFF" section. This also applies to Base Font changes. Any Base Font code in the "OFF" section will be ignored.
  For example, assume that the document is using the default left/right margins (1"). Suppose you created a style with an "ON" code setting the left/right margins to 2" and an "OFF" code setting the margins to 1.5". When the style is turned off, the left/right margins would be 1" because WordPerfect automatically resets what existed before the style and ignored the "OFF" code of 1.5".
- When you use a paired style, WordPerfect inserts a [Style On] code and a [Style Off] code into the document. The [Style On] code and the [Style Off] code operate like the underline and bold codes—they surround the affected text. Therefore, the codes in a paired style only influence the part of the document between the "ON" and "OFF" codes.

How to Create an Outline Style

1. Press *Style* (**Alt-F8**)

    The Style List screen appears. Your screen should look like one of the two following screens:

Figure 3.10
Empty Style List screen

```
Styles


   Name        Type      Description










1 On; 2 Off; 3 Create; 4 Edit; 5 Delete; 6 Save; 7 Retrieve; 8 Update: 1
```

Figure 3.11
Style List screen with LIBRARY.STY

```
Styles


   Name        Type      Description

   Bibliogrphy Paired    Bibliography
   Doc Init    Paired    Initialize Document Style
   Document    Outline   Document Style
   Pleading    Open      Header for numbered pleading paper
   Right Par   Outline   Right-Aligned Paragraph Numbers
   Tech Init   Open      Initialize Technical Style
   Technical   Outline   Technical Document Style


1 On; 2 Off; 3 Create; 4 Edit; 5 Delete; 6 Save; 7 Retrieve; 8 Update: 1
```

If the list is empty (first screen), continue with Step 2. If the list is not empty (second screen), you are looking at a list of styles in a style library. You will first need to delete the listed styles. Deleting the styles from this list only deletes them from the current document; it does not delete them permanently.

27

WordPerfect Styles Made Easy

To delete the styles from the list:

- Highlight a style name
- Press **D**elete (5)
- Press **D**efinition Only (3)

Repeat these three steps until the list is empty.

For more information on style libraries, see Lesson 5, "Saving Styles." For more information on deleting styles, see Lesson 6, "Other Operations." For practice in using the Paragraph Number Definition menu to create an outline style, see Lesson 7, "Practice Exercises."

2. Choose **C**reate (3)

   The Style Edit screen appears:

Figure 3.12
Empty Style Edit screen

```
Styles: Edit

    1 - Name

    2 - Type          Paired

    3 - Description

    4 - Codes

    5 - Enter         HRt


Selection: 0
```

3. Choose **T**ype (2)

   The following menu appears at the bottom of the screen:

   Type: **1 P**aired; **2 O**pen; **3** Outline: **0**

4. Choose Ou**t**line (3)

   In the lower left-hand corner of the screen the following prompt appears:

   Name:

5. Type a style name and press **Enter**

   A style name can have up to 12 characters, including spaces. The style name that you type will be for all outline levels.

28

In the lower left-hand corner of the screen the following prompt appears:

Level Number (1-8):

6. Type **1** (do not press **Enter**)

Figure 3.13
Outline Style Edit screen

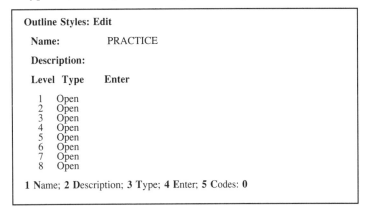

```
Outline Styles: Edit

  Name:            PRACTICE

  Description:

  Level  Type        Enter

     1   Open
     2   Open
     3   Open
     4   Open
     5   Open
     6   Open
     7   Open
     8   Open

  1 Name; 2 Description; 3 Type; 4 Enter; 5 Codes: 0
```

7. Choose **D**escription (2)

   The cursor moves past "Description."

8. Type a description and press **Enter**

   The description can be up to 54 characters, including spaces. The description should contain either an indication of the contents of the style or how the style will be used. It is also a good practice to include the current date as a part of the description. If the style is changed later, remember to change the date included in the description. A good description helps to identify the style.

9. Create either open or paired styles for each level (see the sections earlier in this lesson on how to create open styles and how to create paired styles)

   Start with level 1 since it is already highlighted. Choose **T**ype (3), then choose **P**aired (1) or **O**pen (2). If Paired, choose **E**nter (4), then choose **H**Rt (1), O**ff** (2), or Off/**O**n (3). Choose **C**odes (5) and insert whatever codes you want for that level. After finishing with level 1, use the **Down Arrow** to move the highlight to level 2. Continue setting up the styles for each level.

NOTE

10. Press *Exit* (**F7**) twice

The first *Exit* returns you to the Style List screen.

The second *Exit* returns you to your document.

NOTE: Do not clear your screen at this point or you will lose the style that you created. You must save either the document or the style. For more information see Lesson 5, "Saving Styles."

Lesson 3 Summary

Creating an Open Style

Press *Style* (**Alt-F8**)

Choose Create (3)

Choose Type (2)

Choose Open (2)

Choose Name (1)

Type a Style Name

Press **Enter**

Choose Description (3)

Type a Style Description

Press **Enter**

Choose Codes (4)

Enter the Formatting Codes

Press *Exit* (**F7**) three times

Creating a Paired Style

Press *Style* (**Alt-F8**)

Choose Create (3)

Choose Name (1)

Type a Style Name

Press **Enter**

Choose Description (3)

Type a Style Description

Press **Enter**

Choose Enter (5)

Choose 1, 2, or 3

Choose Codes (4)

Enter the Formatting Codes

Press *Exit* (**F7**) three times

Creating an Outline Style

Press *Style* (**Alt-F8**)

Choose Create (3)

Choose Type (2)

Choose Outline (3)

Type a Style Name

Press **Enter**

Type **1**

Press **Enter**

Choose Description (2)

Type a Style Description

Press **Enter**

Create Open or Paired Styles for all levels

Press *Exit* (**F7**) twice

Notes

Notes

LESSON

4

Using Styles

Using Open Styles

Using a style involves selecting the style's name from a list of styles. This list of styles is called a style library. For more information on style libraries, see Lesson 5, "Saving Styles."

Before selecting a style, it is very important that you place your cursor where you want the style to take effect. For example, to use an open style to affect an entire document, make sure that the cursor is at the beginning of the document. An open style turned on at the end of a document would be useless.

Selecting an open style and turning it on will cause a style code [Open Style: STYLE NAME] to be inserted at the location of the cursor. An open style affects everything in a document from the location of the style code to the end of the document unless another code change overrides it. An open style is not turned off.

Highlighting a style code in *Reveal Codes* (**Alt-F3** or **F11**) causes it to expand to show the contents of the style. For example, highlighting the open style code [Open Style: STYLE NAME] would expand the code so that it might appear as follows: [Open Style: STYLE NAME; [T/B Mar: 1",3"][L/R Mar: 1.5",1.5"][Font: Courier 10cpi]].

How to Select an Open Style

1. Press *Style* (**Alt-F8**)

   The Style List screen appears. Your screen should look like one of the two following screens:

Figure 4.1

Empty Style List screen

```
Styles


Name       Type    Description










1 On; 2 Off; 3 Create; 4 Edit; 5 Delete; 6 Save; 7 Retrieve; 8 Update: 1
```

Figure 4.2

Style List screen with LIBRARY. STY

```
Styles


Name       Type     Description

Bibliogrphy  Paired   Bibliography
Doc Init     Paired   Initialize Document Style
Document     Outline  Document Style
Pleading     Open     Header for numbered pleading paper
Right Par    Outline  Right-Aligned Paragraph Numbers
Tech Init    Open     Initialize Technical Style
Technical    Outline  Technical Document Style


1 On; 2 Off; 3 Create; 4 Edit; 5 Delete; 6 Save; 7 Retrieve; 8 Update: 1
```

   If the style you want is listed, jump to Step 6. If you do not see the style you want, or if the list is empty, continue with Step 2.

2. Choose **R**etrieve (7)

Figure 4.3
Retrieving Styles screen

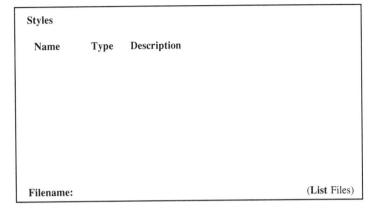

You need to retrieve the style library file that contains the particular style you want to use. For more information about style libraries, see Lesson 5, "Saving Styles."

At this point, you can type the name of the style library. Notice, however, that in the lower right-hand corner WordPerfect lets you know you can use *List* (**F5**) to see your style library file list.

3. Press *List* (**F5**) and press **Enter**

   If this does not produce a list of your style library files (files with a .STY or .WPS extension), something may be wrong with your setup. See the sections "Checking the Present Style Setup" and "Changing the Style Setup" in Lesson 5.

4. Highlight the name of a style library

5. Choose **R**etrieve (1)

   NOTE: You cannot use the **R**etrieve (1) option in *List* (**F5**) to retrieve a style library file unless you have first accessed it through *Styles* (**Alt-F8**).

6. Highlight a style name

   If you want to use a macro to select a style, you need to use Name Search (N) or *Search* (**F2**) to highlight the name of the style.

7. Choose **O**n (1)

NOTE

Using Paired Styles

Using a style involves selecting the style's name from a list of styles. This list of styles is called a style library. For more information on style libraries, see Lesson 5, "Saving Styles."

Before selecting a style, it is very important that you place your cursor where you want the style to take effect. A paired style is turned on just before you type the text to be affected by the style.

You can use paired styles with or without *Block* (**Alt-F4** or **F12**). If you have not yet typed the text, the procedure is

- turn on the style
- type the text you want the style to affect
- turn off the style

If you have already typed the text, the procedure is

- block the text
- select the style

This turns the style on at the beginning of the block and off at the end of the block.

Selecting a paired style inserts into the document both an "ON" code [Style On: STYLE NAME] and an "OFF" code [Style Off: STYLE NAME]. This is the same procedure WordPerfect uses with Underline and Bold. This means you can turn off a paired style by using the **Right Arrow** to move beyond the "OFF" code.

Highlighting a style code in *Reveal Codes* (**Alt-F3** or **F11**) causes it to expand to show the contents of the style.

How to Turn On a Paired Style

1. Press *Style* (**Alt-F8**)

   The Style List screen appears. Your screen should look like one of the two following screens:

Figure 4.4

Empty Style List screen

```
┌─────────────────────────────────────────────────────────────┐
│  Styles                                                       │
│                                                               │
│     Name        Type      Description                         │
│                                                               │
│                                                               │
│                                                               │
│                                                               │
│                                                               │
│                                                               │
│                                                               │
│  1 On; 2 Off; 3 Create; 4 Edit; 5 Delete; 6 Save; 7 Retrieve; 8 Update: 1  │
└─────────────────────────────────────────────────────────────┘
```

Figure 4.5

Style List screen with LIBRARY.STY

```
┌─────────────────────────────────────────────────────────────┐
│  Styles                                                       │
│                                                               │
│     Name        Type      Description                         │
│                                                               │
│   Bibliogrphy  Paired    Bibliography                         │
│   Doc Init     Paired    Initialize Document Style            │
│   Document     Outline   Document Style                       │
│   Pleading     Open      Header for numbered pleading paper    │
│   Right Par    Outline   Right-Aligned Paragraph Numbers      │
│   Tech Init    Open      Initialize Technical Style           │
│   Technical    Outline   Technical Document Style             │
│                                                               │
│  1 On; 2 Off; 3 Create; 4 Edit; 5 Delete; 6 Save; 7 Retrieve; 8 Update: 1  │
└─────────────────────────────────────────────────────────────┘
```

If the style you want is listed, jump to Step 6. If you do not see the style you want, or if the list is empty, continue with Step 2.

2. Choose **R**etrieve (7)

Figure 4.6
Retrieving Styles screen

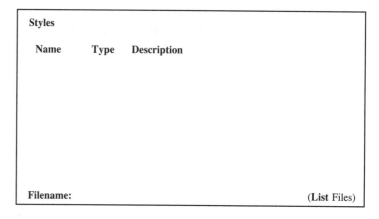

You need to retrieve the style library file that contains the particular style you want to use. For more information about style libraries, see Lesson 5, "Saving Styles."

At this point, you can type the name of the style library. Notice, however, that in the lower right-hand corner WordPerfect lets you know you can use *List* (**F5**) to see your style library file list.

3. Press *List* (**F5**) and press **Enter**

If this does not produce a list of your style library files (files with a .STY or .WPS extension), something may be wrong with your setup. See the sections "Checking the Present Style Setup" and "Changing the Style Setup" in Lesson 5.

4. Highlight the name of a style library

5. Choose **R**etrieve (1)

NOTE: You cannot use the **R**etrieve (1) option in *List* (**F5**) to retrieve a style library file unless you have first accessed it through *Styles* (**Alt-F8**).

6. Highlight a style name

If you want to use a macro to select a style, you need to use Name Search (N) or *Search* (**F2**) to highlight the name of the style.

7. Choose **O**n (1)

NOTE

How to Turn Off a Paired Style

1. If you chose Enter (5) set to <u>H</u>Rt (1)

   Press *Style* (**Alt-F8**)

   Choose O<u>f</u>f (2)

2. If you chose Enter (5) set to O<u>f</u>f (2)

   Press **Enter**

3. If you chose Enter (5) set to Off/<u>O</u>n (3)

   Turn off the style in one of two ways:

   • Press *Style* (**Alt-F8**), choose O<u>f</u>f (2) or
   • Press **Enter**, **Backspace**, type **Y** to confirm deletion

NOTE

NOTE: Regardless of how the **Enter** key was designated, a paired style can always be turned off by moving the cursor beyond the "OFF" code [Style Off: STYLE NAME].

Using Outline Styles

Using an outline style requires a different procedure than using an open or paired style. In fact, you cannot select an outline style from the style menu [*Style* (**Alt-F8**)]. You can only use an outline style from the Paragraph Numbering Definition menu [*Outline* (**Shift-F5**), **D**efine (6)].

Before selecting a style, it is very important that you place your cursor where you want the style to take effect. Otherwise, you will get results you did not intend.

Selecting an outline style will cause a [Par Num Def: STYLE NAME] code to be inserted at the location of the cursor. The codes for all levels of the outline will be in effect until the outline feature is turned off. That particular outline style will be valid for all paragraph numbering and outlining until another [Par Num Def] code is encountered.

Highlighting an outline style code in *Reveal Codes* (**Alt-F3** or **F11**) does not cause it to expand the way it does for open or paired styles since an outline style can contain up to eight different styles.

The next two pages describe how to use an outline style, that is, how to designate that a certain style be used for both the paragraph numbering feature and the outline feature. It is assumed that the reader already knows how to use WordPerfect's outline feature.

How to Select an Outline Style

1. Press *Date/Outline* (**Shift-F5**)

   The following menu appears at the bottom of the screen.

   > **1** Date **T**ext; **2** Date **C**ode; **3** Date **F**ormat; **4** **O**utline;
   > **5** **P**ara Num; **6** **D**efine: 0

2. Choose **D**efine (6)

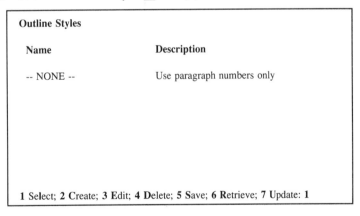

Figure 4.7
Paragraph Number Definition screen

3. Choose Outline Style **N**ame (9)

Outline Styles

Name	Description
-- NONE --	Use paragraph numbers only

1 Select; **2** Create; **3** Edit; **4** Delete; **5** Save; **6** Retrieve; **7** Update: 1

Figure 4.8
Outline Styles Style List screen

4. Choose **R**etrieve (6)

   In the bottom left-hand corner, the following prompt appears:

   Filename:

At this point, you can type the name of the style library. However, in the lower right-hand corner WordPerfect has the following prompt:

(**List** Files)

This lets you know you can use *List* (**F5**) to see your style library file list.

5. Press *List* (**F5**) and **Enter**

   If this does not produce a list of your style library files (files with a .STY or .WPS extension), something may be wrong with your setup. See the sections "Checking the Present Style Setup" and "Changing the Style Setup" in Lesson 5.

6. Highlight the name of a style library

7. Choose **R**etrieve (1)

NOTE

   NOTE: You cannot use the **R**etrieve (1) option in *List* (**F5**) to retrieve a style library file unless you have first accessed it through *Styles* (**Alt-F8**).

8. Highlight a style name

   If you want to use a macro to select a style, you need to use **N**ame Search (N) or *Search* (**F2**) to highlight the name of the style.

9. Choose Se**l**ect (1)

   You are returned to the paragraph number definition menu. The name of the selected style appears after "9 - Outline Style Name."

Reminder:
To start outlining, press Enter.

10. Press *Exit* (**F7**)

11. Choose **O**utline (4)

12. Choose **O**n (1)

Lesson 4 Summary

Using Open Styles

(with default styles)

Press *Style* (**Alt-F8**)
Highlight a Style Name
Choose **O**n (1)

(without default styles)

Press *Style* (**Alt-F8**)
Choose **R**etrieve (7)
Press *List* (**F5**)
Press **Enter**
Highlight a Style Library Name
Choose **R**etrieve (1)
Highlight the Style Name
Choose **O**n (1)

Using Outline Styles

Press *Outline* (**Shift-F5**)
Choose **D**efine (6)
Choose Style **N**ame (9)
Choose **R**etrieve (6)
Press *List* (**F5**)
Press **Enter**
Highlight a Style Library Name
Choose **R**etrieve (1)
Highlight the Style Name
Choose Sel**e**ct (1)
Press *Exit* (**F7**)
Choose **O**utline (4)
Choose **O**n (1)

Using Paired Styles

Turning On
(with default styles)

Press *Style* (**Alt-F8**)
Highlight a Style Name
Choose **O**n (1)

(without default styles)

Press *Style* (**Alt-F8**)
Choose **R**etrieve (7)
Press *List* (**F5**)
Press **Enter**
Highlight a Style Library Name
Choose **R**etrieve (1)
Highlight a Style Name
Choose **O**n (1)

Turning Off

Press **Right Arrow**
(to move past the "OFF" code)
or
Press *Style* (**Alt-F8**)
Highlight a style name
Choose O**f**f (2)

Notes

Notes

LESSON

5

Saving Styles

Ways That Styles are Saved

Saved with the Document

Styles are automatically saved when you save the document. If you need a style only for the current document, you don't need to do anything special to save it. Whether you use the style or not, the style definition becomes a part of the current document.

If you create a style and then don't save the document, the style definition is lost. Any changes you make to a style will not be permanent until you save the document.

Saved in a Style Library

If the style can be used in a number of documents, the style should be saved separately from the document. Styles are not saved as individual files; they are saved in style libraries. A style library consists of individual styles that have been combined and saved under one name.

You *can* save a style by itself (in a library of one), but after you work with styles for a while you will realize that there are many advantages to grouping styles into categories. The grouping is usually done according to the type of document in which the styles will be used.

Checking the Present Style Setup

Before you save a style, you should know where WordPerfect is going to store it. Find the location of style files and see if a default style library is designated by following these steps. Make sure you have a blank screen before starting.

1. Press *Style* (**Alt-F8**)

   If there are files listed, you have a default style library file designated. If you have a default style library listed (other than LIBRARY.STY), you may want to see which styles are contained in the library. The contents of LIBRARY.STY are explained later in this lesson.

2. Choose **R**etrieve (7)

3. Press *List* (**F5**)

   Look at the designation in the lower left-hand corner. This tells you the subdirectory where WordPerfect will save the styles. Make a note of the subdirectory listed (if not C:\WP51\STYLES). You will need that information later.

   If it reads C:\WP51*.*, your style files will be intermixed with all of WordPerfect's files. Such a location is not recommended because it makes locating a particular file very difficult.

4. Press *Cancel* (**F1**) twice

   NOTE: Remember to clear the screen before working on a document or the styles will become a part of that document.

NOTE

Changing the Style Setup

The following instructions are based on two recommendations. First, it is suggested that C:\WP51\STYLES be the default directory in which WordPerfect saves all styles. Second, you should not designate a default style library; pressing *Style* (**Alt-F8**) should not automatically produce a list of styles. Having a default style library increases the size of every saved document.

Changing the style setup involves the following steps:

- Locate the STYLES subdirectory. There is no need to create a STYLES subdirectory if one already exists.
- Create the STYLES subdirectory, if it does not already exist.
- Move all the present style files to the STYLES subdirectory.
- Change the defaults in setup, designating the newly created subdirectory as the default style directory (not library).

Locating the STYLES Subdirectory

1. Press *List* (**F5**)
2. Type **C:\WP51*.** and press **Enter**

   Typing the *. will produce a list of subdirectories.
3. Look at the list of subdirectories to see if the subdirectory STYLES exists
4. Press *Exit* (**F7**) to return to the document screen

Creating the STYLES Subdirectory

1. Press *List* (**F5**) and press **Enter**
2. Choose **O**ther Directory (7)
3. Type **C:\WP51\STYLES** and press **Enter**

   The following prompt appears in the lower left-hand corner:

   Create C:\WP51\STYLES? No (Yes)
4. Type **Y**
5. Press *Exit* (**F7**)

Moving Files to the STYLES Subdirectory

1. Press *List* (**F5**)
2. Type **C:\WP51*.STY** and press **Enter**

   This will produce a list of all style files that exist in the WP51 subdirectory. If your default style directory was not C:\WP51, type the subdirectory that you discovered in "Checking the Present Style Setup," Step (3) above.
3. Press *Mark Text* (**Alt-F5**)

   This marks all the files. Notice the * before each filename.

4. Choose **M**ove/Rename (3)

   The following prompt appears:

   Move marked files? No (Yes)

5. Type **Y**

   The following prompt appears:

   Move marked files to:

6. Type **C:\WP51\STYLES** and press **Enter**

7. Press *Exit* (**F7**)

Changing the Defaults

1. Press *Setup* (**Shift-F1**)

2. Choose **L**ocation of Files (6)

3. Choose **S**tyle Files (5)

4. Type **C:\WP51\STYLES** and press **Enter**

5. Use **Ctrl-End** to delete the second line "Library Filename."

   If you delete the style library filename in setup, you are not deleting the style library, you are just saying you don't want it to be the default.

How to Save a Style Library

Now that you know where WordPerfect will save your style library files, you can save your styles.

1. Press *Style* (**Alt-F8**)

   A list of the styles for the current document appears.

2. Press **S**ave (6)

   NOTE: You will save all the listed styles, not just the style that is highlighted.

   A prompt appears, asking for a name for the style library:

   Filename:

3. Type a style library filename and press **Enter**

   The filename must conform to the same DOS filename rules as document names (up to 8 characters in the root and a

NOTE

maximum of three characters for the extension). It is suggested that .STY (Style) or .WPS (WordPerfect Style) be used for the extension in order to identify the file.

The following prompt may appear asking if you want to replace an existing style library file.

Replace C:\WP51\STYLES\FILENAME.STY? No (Yes)

Answer Yes (Y) or No (N)

If you answer Y, it replaces ("overwrites") the existing style library with the list of styles on the screen. If you answer N, you must give a different name for the style library.

WordPerfect's Ready-Made Styles

Figure 5.1
Style List Screen (with LIBRARY.STY)

```
Styles


Name        Type     Description

Bibliogrphy  Paired   Bibliography
Doc Init     Paired   Initialize Document Style
Document     Outline  Document Style
Pleading     Open     Header for numbered pleading paper
Right Par     Outline  Right-Aligned Paragraph Numbers
Tech Init     Open     Initialize Technical Style
Technical     Outline  Technical Document Style




1 On; 2 Off; 3 Create; 4 Edit; 5 Delete; 6 Save; 7 Retrieve; 8 Update: 1
```

WordPerfect supplies a number of ready-made styles that you can use. Here is a brief description of WordPerfect's style library (LIBRARY.STY).

Bibliography: Used to create hanging paragraphs; **Enter** key is Off/On; text is automatically indented after the first line; entries are double spaced

Doc Init: Used to set up the Document outline style; contains the TofC definition in the "ON" section and new page number in the "OFF" section; when you generate a TofC, it is put between the "ON" and "OFF" codes

Document:	Contains paragraph numbering and TofC codes; used to insert chapter headings and subheadings; automatically defines a table of contents and marks the headings
Pleading:	Has a double vertical line and numbering at the left; fixes line height at 6 lines per inch; sets top and bottom margins; codes are in a header so they affect every page
Right Par:	Has eight levels of outline with right-aligned paragraph numbers; has two HRt's separate levels with a blank line; **Enter** key is Off/On; right-aligned paragraph numbers allow the periods to line up
Tech Init:	Used to set up the technical outline style and turn on the outline; also used to create a technical document
Technical:	Used to format technical papers

It may be helpful to look at the codes contained in these styles in order to assist you in developing your own styles or to determine whether you want to use any of the provided styles. To see the codes contained in any of these styles, make sure you start with a blank screen and do the following.

1. Press *Style* (**Alt-F8**)
2. Choose **R**etrieve (7)
3. Type **LIBRARY.STY** and press **Enter**
4. Highlight any one of the styles
5. Choose **E**dit (4)
6. Choose **C**odes (4)
7. Look at the codes
8. Press *Exit* (**F7**) three times

   NOTE: Remember to clear the screen before working on a document or the styles will become a part of that document.

NOTE

Customizing Your Own Style Library

Once you learn how useful styles are, you will create a number of styles. Here are some suggestions for creating customized style libraries.

1. Use one or many style libraries

    If you use only one style library, make it the default (put it in setup). If you use multiple style libraries, designate only the style directory in setup, but not a filename (leave the second line blank).

2. Combine style libraries

    One way to create styles is to start on a blank screen, create a lot of styles, and save each style to its own file. At some point you will, of course, want to look over the created styles, decide on some organization, and use the style retrieve function to get them together into collections. For information on retrieving, see Lesson 6, "Other Operations." After saving the combined style library, delete the individual ones that are no longer needed.

    The style library names should reflect the types of documents in which the styles will be used. Examples: BUSINESS.STY; PERSONAL.STY; AUTHOR.STY; THESIS.STY; NEWSLTR.STY; ACCOUNTS.STY.

Lesson 5 Summary

Ways That Styles are Saved

Styles are automatically saved with the document. To use a style in a number of documents, save a style in a style library. A style library is a group of styles saved under one name.

Checking the Present Style Setup

It is necessary to know whether there is a default style library designated and where WordPerfect will store the styles.

Changing the Style Setup

The STYLES subdirectory must be located or created and all present style files moved into it. Then Setup is used to change the defaults.

How to Save a Style Library

When a list of styles is displayed on the Style List screen, choosing Save will save all the styles listed.

WordPerfect's Ready-Made Styles

WordPerfect provides a file called LIBRARY.STY that contains two paired, two open, and three outline styles.

Customizing Your Own Style Library

Once a number of styles have been created, they should be combined with related styles to produce various business and personal formats grouped together.

Notes

Notes

_____

_____

_____

_____

_____

_____

_____

_____

_____

_____

_____

_____

_____

_____

_____

_____

_____

_____

_____

_____

_____

_____

_____

6

Other Operations

Editing a Style

Editing a style usually involves changing the codes, text, or graphics that are contained in the style. Normally you do not want to change a style's name, particularly one that is in use. However, if you do rename a style, WordPerfect displays the following prompt:

Rename styles in Document? No (Yes)

You should answer Y (YES). If you answer N (NO), the link between the style code and the style definition is lost. Therefore, the styles in the document would not reflect any changes made to the newly named style.

If your style contains text, you can use the speller and thesaurus on the style codes screen.

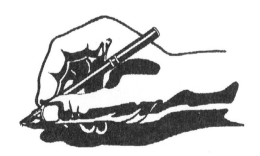

How to Edit a Style

1. Press *Style* (**Alt-F8**)
2. Choose **R**etrieve (7)
3. Press *List* (**F5**) and press **Enter**
4. Highlight a Style Library Filename
5. Choose **R**etrieve (1)
6. Highlight a Style Name
7. Choose **E**dit (4)
8. Choose **C**odes (4)
9. Edit the style codes

   Make any additions, deletions, or changes desired.
10. Press *Exit* (**F7**)
11. Choose **D**escription (3)
12. Edit the Description

    Make any necessary changes in the description (including the date) to reflect the current contents of the style.
13. Press *Exit* (**F7**) twice

Deleting a Style

Because of the way that styles are saved, it is especially important to delete old, unneeded styles from style libraries. If you don't, every document's size is needlessly increased.

When you delete a style from the list, it affects only the current document, not the style library (unless you re-save the new list using the same style library filename).

There are many ways to delete styles and style library files:

- delete only one usage of a style
- delete all usages of a style
- delete a style from a style library
- delete a style library

Deleting Only One Usage of a Style

If it is an open style, go into *Reveal Codes* (**Alt-F3** or **F11**) and delete the [Open Style] code. If it is a paired style, delete either the [Style On] or [Style Off] code from the document. You can use *Search* (**F2**) to locate these codes: [Open Style], [Style On], or [Style Off].

Deleting All Usages of a Style

1. Press *Style* (**Alt-F8**)
2. Highlight the name of the style
3. Choose **D**elete (5)
4. Choose 1, 2, or 3

   Leaving Codes (1) deletes the style but converts all the style codes into regular WordPerfect codes.

   Including Codes (2) deletes the style and the codes.

   Definition Only (3) deletes the definition only. Any style codes in the document are unaffected.

5. Press *Exit* (**F7**)

Deleting a Style from a Style Library

1. Press *Style* (**Alt-F8**)
2. Choose **R**etrieve (7)
3. Press *List* (**F5**) and press **Enter**
4. Highlight a Style Library filename
5. Choose **R**etrieve (1)
6. Highlight a Style Name
7. Choose **D**elete (5 or D)
8. Choose **I**ncluding Codes (2)
9. Choose **S**ave (6)
10. Type the same Style Library filename

11. Type **Y**

Answering Y (YES) replaces the old version with the new version. This will overwrite the style library file, thus eliminating the deleted style from the style library.

12. Press *Exit* (**F7**)

Deleting a Style Library

1. Press *List* (**F5**)

2. Type **C:\WP51\STYLES** and press **Enter**

If STYLES is not your default style directory (where the style library files are saved), then type the name of the subdirectory where your styles are located. See the sections "Checking the Present Style Setup" and "Changing the Style Setup" in Lesson 5.

3. Highlight the name of the style library to be deleted

4. Choose **D**elete (2)

The following prompt appears:

Delete C:\WP51\STYLES\FILENAME.STY? No (Yes)

5. Type **Y**

This confirms that you want to delete the style library file.

6. Press *Exit* (**F7**)

WordPerfect Can Reconstruct a Style List

It is best to delete all unused styles from the style list so that they will not be saved along with the document. It is possible, however, that you have a long list of styles and can't remember which are being used in the current document. If you delete the styles in use, WordPerfect will reconstruct the style list to include only those currently in use.

To have WordPerfect reconstruct a list of only the styles being used in the current document, do the following. Delete all of the styles using the **D**elete (5), **D**efinition Only (3) option, return to your document and move the cursor through it (use **Home, Home, Up Arrow** then **Home, Home, Down Arrow**). WordPerfect has now reconstructed the style list, but all the descriptions are lost.

Retrieving and Updating Styles

Retrieving Styles

Always save the style library or document before retrieving other styles. In case you make an error, you can always get back what you had before.

When you use **R**etrieve (7) on the Style List menu, you can retrieve styles from a style library or from another document. In the latter case, the retrieve option brings in the styles from the document, not the document itself.

Retrieving only brings in a copy of the styles from a style library. If you make changes, you would need to re-save in order to change the styles in the style library.

How to Retrieve a Style Library

1. Press *Style* (**Alt-F8**)

2. Choose **R**etrieve (7)

3. Press *List* (**F5**) and press **Enter**

4. Highlight Style Library filename

5. Choose **R**etrieve (1)

    A list of styles appears on the screen unless there is a name duplication problem. If the name of one of the styles in the current document and the name of one of the styles in the retrieved style library is the same, WordPerfect displays the following prompt:

    Style(s) already exist. Replace? No (Yes)

    If you answer Y (YES), WordPerfect overwrites the style of the same name (i.e., replaces the style in the document with the one from the style library). If you answer N (NO), WordPerfect reads in only those styles with different names.

6. Press *Exit* (**F7**)

WordPerfect Styles Made Easy

Consolidating Styles

If you find that you have too many style library files, determine which ones you want to group together. Combine them as follows:

1. Press *Style* (**Alt-F8**)
2. Choose **R**etrieve (7)
3. Type a Style Library filename and press **Enter**
4. Repeat Steps 2 and 3 as many times as necessary
5. Choose **S**ave (6)
6. Type a Style Library filename

   Be sure that the name you use is a new name that will not interfere with any present files.
7. Press *Exit* (**F7**)

After combining a number of smaller style library files, you will need to delete these unneeded files. Here is a quick way to delete them:

1. Press *List* (**F5**)
2. Type **C:\WP51\STYLES** and press **Enter**
3. Highlight a Style Library to be deleted
4. Press * (asterisk)
5. Repeat Steps 3 and 4 as many times as necessary
6. Choose **D**elete (2)

   The following prompt appears:

   Delete marked files? No (Yes)
7. Type **Y**

   The following prompt appears:

   Marked files will be deleted. Continue? No (Yes)
8. Type **Y**

   When the operation is finished, the menu reappears at the bottom of the screen.
9. Press *Exit* (**F7**)

Updating Styles

Always save the document you are working on before using update. Update will automatically overwrite the styles without asking for confirmation.

Update copies the styles from the default style library to the document on the screen. It does not ask for confirmation to overwrite because it assumes you want to overwrite and update the styles.

Update works only with the default style library. If you don't have a default style library designated, you won't need to use update. In fact, without a default style library, choosing Update (8) from the Styles List menu doesn't do anything.

Differences Between Retrieve and Update

Name of Style Library
>Retrieve: Need to designate the style library filename
>Update: Always uses the default style library

Overwrite Warning
>Retrieve: Warns of overwrite; asks for confirmation
>Update: No warning; assumes you want to overwrite

Lesson 6 Summary

Editing a Style

Press *Style* (**Alt-F8**)
Choose **R**etrieve (7)
Press *List* (**F5**)
Press **Enter**
Highlight a Style Library Filename
Choose **R**etrieve (1)
Highlight a Style Name
Choose **E**dit (4)
Choose **C**odes (4)
Edit the style codes
Press *Exit* (**F7**)
Choose **D**escription (3)
Edit the description
Press *Exit* (**F7**) twice

Deleting a Style

There are many ways to delete styles and style libraries: delete only one usage of a style, delete all usages of a style, delete a style from a style library, delete a style library.

Retrieving and Updating Styles

Retrieve is used to bring in styles from a style library or from another document. If there is a name duplication problem, WordPerfect will ask for confirmation before overwriting the style. Update uses only a default style library and does not warn of overwriting.

Notes

Notes

_____

_____

_____

_____

_____

_____

_____

_____

_____

_____

_____

_____

_____

_____

_____

_____

_____

_____

_____

_____

_____

_____

LESSON

7

Practice Exercises

For the purposes of these exercises, you will save most of these styles separately, in a style library of one. For information on saving styles see the section "Ways That Styles are Saved" in Lesson 5.

You should always start with a blank screen and be sure to clear the screen afterwards before working on any document.

After you have done all the practice exercises, you will want to customize these styles for your own use and group related styles together. See the section "Combining Style Libraries" in Lesson 5.

Creating a Style for a Title

1. Press *Style* (**Alt-F8**)

2. Choose <u>C</u>reate (3)

3. Choose <u>N</u>ame (1)

4. Type **TITLE** and press **Enter**

5. Choose <u>D</u>escription (3)

6. Type **CENTERED, BOLDED, VERY LARGE** and press **Enter**

7. Choose <u>E</u>nter (5)

8. Choose O<u>f</u>f (2)

9. Choose <u>C</u>odes (4)

10. Enter the codes

    (a) Press *Center* (**Shift-F6**)
    (b) Press *Bold* (**F6**)
    (c) Press *Font* (**Ctrl-F8**)
    (d) Choose <u>S</u>ize (1)
    (e) Choose <u>V</u>ry Large (6)
    (f) Press **Right Arrow**
    (g) Press **Enter** twice

11. Press *Exit* (**F7**) twice

12. Choose <u>S</u>ave (6)

13. Type **TITLE.STY** and press **Enter**

14. Press *Exit* (**F7**)

15. Press *Exit* (**F7**), type **N**, type **N** to clear the screen

Using a Style for a Title

Using a style for the title not only makes the job of formatting easier, it provides for consistency. If everyone in the office uses the same style for each title, then every title will have the same formatting. This results in documents that create a better impression. More importantly, if someone decides to change the appearance of the titles, revising a style is easy.

This sample style has two lines following the title. If you always want to have more or less than two, just change the number of HRt's that follow the Comment code.

THE CODES FOR "TITLE" LOOK LIKE THIS:

[Center][BOLD][VRY LARGE][Comment][HRt][HRt]

Creating a Style for a Bulleted List

1. Press *Style* (**Alt-F8**)

2. Choose **C**reate (3)

3. Choose **N**ame (1)

4. Type **LIST** and press **Enter**

5. Choose **D**escription (3)

6. Type **USED FOR BULLETED LIST** and press **Enter**

7. Choose **E**nter (5)

8. Choose Off/**O**n (3)

9. Choose **C**odes (4)

10. Enter the codes

    (a)   Press →*Indent* (**F4**)
    (b)   Press **Ctrl-V**
    (c)   Type **4,0** and press **Enter**
    (d)   Press →*Indent* (**F4**)
    (e)   Press **Right Arrow**
    (f)   Press **Enter** twice

11. Press *Exit* (**F7**) twice

12. Choose **S**ave (6)

13. Type **LIST.STY** and press **Enter**

14. Press *Exit* (**F7**)

15. Press *Exit* (**F7**), type **N**, type **N** to clear the screen

Using the Bulleted List Style

- Using bulleted lists can call attention to important information. This style allows you to easily prepare a list of items with the attention-getting bullet in front of each.

- **Ctrl-V** accesses WordPerfect's Compose feature. If you prefer not to use a round bullet, change the "4,0" to another symbol. Check the WordPerfect manual for a list of characters that can be used with the Compose feature.

- Note: This style sets the **Enter** key option to "Off/On." Be sure to read the section "How to Turn Off a Paired Style" in Lesson 4, "Using Styles."

THE CODES FOR "LIST" LOOK LIKE THIS:

[→Indent]•[→Indent][Comment][HRt][HRt]

Creating a Style for an Envelope

This style creates the formatting needed to do a 9" x 4" envelope. This one is without a return address to be used with preprinted envelopes. It assumes that you already have a paper size/type defined for a 9" x 4" envelope.

1. Press *Style* (**Alt-F8**)

2. Choose **C**reate (3)

3. Choose **T**ype (2)

4. Choose **O**pen (2)

5. Choose **N**ame (1)

6. Type **ENVELOPE** and press **Enter**

7. Choose **D**escription (3)

8. Type **9x4 ENVELOPE W/O RET. ADD.** and press **Enter**

9. Choose **C**odes (4)

10. Enter the codes

    (a) Press *Format* (**Shift-F8**)
    (b) Choose **P**age (2)
    (c) Choose Paper **S**ize (7)
    (d) Highlight Envelope - Wide
    (e) Choose **S**elect (1)
    (f) Choose **M**argins (5)
    (g) Type **2** and press **Enter**
    (h) Type **0.3** and press **Enter**
    (i) Press **Enter**
    (j) Choose **L**ine (1)
    (k) Choose **M**argins (7)
    (l) Type **4** and press **Enter**
    (m) Type **0.3** and press **Enter**
    (n) Press *Exit* (**F7**)

11. Press *Exit* (**F7**) twice

12. Choose **S**ave (6)

13. Type **ENVELOPE.STY** and press **Enter**

14. Press *Exit* (**F7**)

Once you create this style, producing envelopes is easy.

Jane Martin
1234 State Street
Santa Cruz, NM 57111

THE CODES FOR "ENVELOPE" LOOK LIKE THIS:

[Paper Sz/Typ:9.5" x 4", Envelope][T/B Mar:2", 0.3"]
[L/R Mar:4", 0.3"]

Creating a Style for Hanging Paragraphs

1. Press *Style* (**Alt-F8**)
2. Choose **C**reate (3)
3. Choose **N**ame (1)
4. Type **HANGING INDENT** and press **Enter**
5. Choose **D**escription (3)
6. Type **USED FOR SERIES OF HANGING PARAGRAPHS** and press **Enter**
7. Choose **E**nter (5)
8. Choose Off/**O**n (3)
9. Choose **C**odes (4)
10. Enter the codes
    (a) Press →*Indent* (**F4**)
    (b) Press ←*Margin Release* (**Shift-Tab**)
    (c) Press **Right Arrow**
    (d) Press **Enter** twice
11. Press *Exit* (**F7**) twice
12. Choose **S**ave (6)
13. Type **HANGING.STY** and press **Enter**
14. Press *Exit* (**F7**)
15. Press *Exit* (**F7**), type **N**, type **N** to clear the screen

Using the Hanging Indent Style

The hanging indent (sometimes called an outdent) is used for a paragraph where the first line is to the left of the rest of the paragraph. It is used for many types of documents, including bibliographies.

Using WordPerfect's Indent feature causes a temporary margin to be established. That temporary margin stays in effect until an **Enter** key is pressed. The margin release key (**Shift-Tab**) causes the cursor to move to the left of the margin, either a temporary or a permanent margin.

THE CODES FOR "HANGING" LOOK LIKE THIS:

[→Indent][←Mar Rel][Comment][HRt][HRt]

Creating a Style for a Quotation

1. Press *Style* (**Alt-F8**)

2. Choose <u>C</u>reate (3)

3. Choose <u>N</u>ame (1)

4. Type **QUOTATION** and press **Enter**

5. Choose <u>D</u>escription (3)

6. Type **USED FOR LONG QUOTATIONS** and press **Enter**

7. Choose <u>E</u>nter (5)

8. Choose O<u>f</u>f (2)

9. Choose <u>C</u>odes (4)

10. Enter the codes

    (a) Press →*Indent*← (**Shift-F4**)
    (b) Press *Font* (**Ctrl-F8**)
    (c) Choose <u>A</u>ppearance (2)
    (d) Choose <u>I</u>talc (4)
    (e) Choose *Format* (**Shift-F8**)
    (f) Choose <u>L</u>ine (1)
    (g) Choose Line <u>S</u>pacing (6)
    (h) Type **1** and press **Enter**
    (i) Press *Exit* (**F7**)
    (j) Press **Right Arrow**
    (k) Press **Enter** twice

11. Press *Exit* (**F7**) twice

12. Choose <u>S</u>ave (6)

13. Type **QUOTE.STY** and press **Enter**

14. Press *Exit* (**F7**)

15. Press *Exit* (**F7**), type **N**, type **N** to clear the screen

Using Styles for Long Quotations

Using styles helps the student prepare term papers or theses and helps anyone prepare reports of any kind. The regular text of term papers, theses, or reports is usually double spaced. Long quotations, however, are sometimes single spaced, and indented from both the left and right margin and in italics.

> *Although the primary advantage of styles seems to be how easy revisions can be made, using styles can also speed up the process of formatting. Using styles makes formatting consistent, dependable, and fast![1]*

When the style is turned on, all of the necessary formatting is done instantly. When the style is turned off, all of the formatting reverts back to what was there before the style was used.

THE CODES FOR "QUOTATION" LOOK LIKE THIS:

[→Indent←][ITALC][Ln Spacing:1][Comment][HRt][HRt]

Creating an Outline Style

This practice exercise will create an outline style that bolds the outline level markers and automatically indents after each level.

Outline styles can be created from the Style List screen or from the Paragraph Number Definition menu. However, they can be used only from the latter. This exercise will use the Paragraph Number Definition menu to create the outline style.

1. Press *Outline* (**Shift-F5**)
2. Choose **D**efine (6)
3. Choose Outline Style **N**ame (9)
4. Choose **C**reate (2)
5. Choose **N**ame (1)
6. Type **OUTLINE** and press **Enter**
7. Choose **D**escription (2)
8. Type **BOLD, INDENTED** and press **Enter**

   Level 1 is highlighted.

9. Enter the codes for level 1
   - (a) Choose **T**ype (3)
   - (b) Choose **P**aired (1)
   - (c) Choose **C**odes (5)
   - (d) Press *Block* (**Alt-F4** or **F12**)
   - (e) Press **Right Arrow**
   - (f) Press *Bold* (**F6**)
   - (g) Press →*Indent* (**F4**)
10. Press *Exit* (**F7**)
11. Press **Down Arrow**

    Level 2 is now highlighted.
12. Enter the codes for level 2, and so on.

    Repeat the same procedure used for Level 1 except for this change: Level 2 has one tab before the rest of the codes, Level 3 has two tabs, Level 4 has three tabs, and so on. Continue until all 8 levels have been done.

13. Press *Exit* (**F7**)

14. Choose **S**ave (5)

15. Type **OUTLINE.STY** and press **Enter**

16. Press *Exit* (**F7**) twice

The resulting outline style would look like this:

I.   Level 1

II.   Level 1

      A.   Level 2
      B.   Level 2
           1.   Level 3
           2.   Level 3
      C.   Level 2

III.   Level 1

THE CODES FOR "OUTLINE-LEVEL 1" LOOK LIKE THIS:

[BOLD][Par Num:1][bold][→Indent][Comment]

THE CODES FOR "OUTLINE-LEVEL 2" LOOK LIKE THIS:

[Tab][BOLD][Par Num:2][bold][→Indent][Comment]

THE CODES FOR "OUTLINE-LEVEL 3" LOOK LIKE THIS:

[Tab][Tab][BOLD][Par Num:3][bold][→Indent][Comment]

THE CODES FOR "OUTLINE-LEVEL 4" LOOK LIKE THIS:

[Tab][Tab][Tab][BOLD][Par Num:4][bold]
[→Indent][Comment]

THE CODES FOR "OUTLINE-LEVEL 5" LOOK LIKE THIS:

[Tab][Tab][Tab][Tab][BOLD][Par Num:5][bold]
[→Indent][Comment]

THE CODES FOR "OUTLINE-LEVEL 6" LOOK LIKE THIS:

[Tab][Tab][Tab][Tab][Tab][BOLD][Par Num:6][bold]
[→Indent][Comment]

THE CODES FOR "OUTLINE-LEVEL 7" LOOK LIKE THIS:

[Tab][Tab][Tab][Tab][Tab][Tab][BOLD][Par Num:7]
[bold][→Indent][Comment]

THE CODES FOR "OUTLINE-LEVEL 8" LOOK LIKE THIS:

[Tab][Tab][Tab][Tab][Tab][Tab][Tab][BOLD][Par Num:8]
[bold][→Indent][Comment]

Practice in Editing a Style

In this exercise you are going to edit the style "TITLE" in order to create two other styles—CHAPTER NUMBER and CHAPTER TITLE. These new styles will include markings for a Table of Contents but will not have the two HRt's after the title.

These two styles, along with an open style to do the overall formatting for the document would normally be saved together in one style library. For purposes of this practice, however, you will save these to CHAP-NUM.STY and CHAP-TIT.STY respectively.

Make sure that you start on a blank screen. You do not want changes to the style to affect any document.

THE CODES FOR "CHAPTER NUMBER" LOOK LIKE THIS:
[Center][BOLD][VRY LARGE][Mark:ToC,1][Comment]
[End Mark:ToC,1][HRt][HRt]

THE CODES FOR "CHAPTER TITLE" LOOK LIKE THIS:
[Center][BOLD][VRY LARGE][Mark:ToC,2][Comment]
[End Mark:ToC,2][HRt][HRt]

Imagine you wanted the chapter numbers and chapter titles to appear as follows:

Chapter 1
Introduction

Chapter 2
How to Set Up a Meeting

Chapter 3
The Welcome Process

Chapter 4
Introducing Speakers

Chapter 5
Wrap-Up Procedures

Also, you wanted to use WordPerfect's Table of Contents feature to generate a table of contents like the following:

TABLE OF CONTENTS

Edit "TITLE" to Create "CHAPTER NUMBER"

1. Press *Style* (**Alt-F8**)

2. Choose **R**etrieve (7)

3. Type **TITLE.STY** and press **Enter**

4. Choose **E**dit (4)

5. Choose **C**odes (4)

6. Change the codes

    (a) Press **Right Arrow** three times
    The Comment code is now highlighted.

    (b) Press *Block* (**Alt-F4** or **F12**)

    (c) Press **Right Arrow**

    (d) Press *Mark Text* (**Alt-F5**)
    Prompt reads:
    Mark for: 1 ToC; 2 List; 3 Index; 4 ToA: 0

    (e) Choose To**C** (1)
    Prompt reads: ToC Level:

    (f) Type **1** and press **Enter**

    (g) Press **Delete** once

7. Press *Exit* (**F7**)

8. Choose **N**ame (1)

9. Type **CHAPTER NUMBER** and press **Enter**

   Prompt reads: Rename Styles in Document? No (Yes)

10. Type **N**

11. Choose **D**escription (3)

12. Type **CHAPTER NUMBER WITH ToC MARKING** and press **Enter**

13. Press *Exit* (**F7**)

14. Choose **S**ave (6)

15. Type **CHAP-NUM.STY** and press **Enter**

16. Press *Exit* (**F7**)

17. Press *Exit* (**F7**), type **N**, type **N** to clear the screen

Edit "TITLE" to Create "CHAPTER TITLE"

1. Press *Style* (**Alt-F8**)

2. Choose **R**etrieve (7)

3. Type **TITLE.STY** and press **Enter**

4. Choose **E**dit (4)

5. Choose **C**odes (4)

6. Change the codes

   (a) Press **Right Arrow** three times
   The Comment code is now highlighted.

   (b) Press *Block* (**Alt-F4** or **F12**)

   (c) Press **Right Arrow**

   (d) Press *Mark Text* (**Alt-F5**)
   Prompt reads:
       Mark for: 1 ToC; 2 List; 3 Index; 4 ToA: 0

   (e) Choose To**C** (1)
   Prompt reads: ToC Level:

   (f) Type **2** and press **Enter**

   (g) Press **Delete** once

7. Press *Exit* (**F7**)

8. Choose **N**ame (1)

9. Type **CHAPTER TITLE** and press **Enter**

   Prompt reads: Rename Styles in Document? No (Yes)

10. Type **N**

11. Choose **D**escription (3)

12. Type **CHAPTER TITLE WITH ToC MARKING** and press **Enter**

13. Press *Exit* (**F7**)

14. Choose **S**ave (6)

15. Type **CHAP-TIT.STY** and press **Enter**

16. Press *Exit* (**F7**)

17. Press *Exit* (**F7**), type **N**, type **N** to clear the screen

Creating Letterhead Styles

The following instructions are to be used to create any of the four letterhead examples that follow. The only differences occur in the name, the description and the codes. The specific codes for each of the four letterhead styles follow these general instructions. A sample of what the letterhead looks like, along with how the codes look on the Style Codes screen is included.

1. Press *Style* (**Alt-F8**)

2. Choose **C**reate (3)

3. Choose **T**ype (2)

4. Choose **O**pen (2)

5. Choose **N**ame (1)

6. Type the style name and press **Enter**

   Type LETTERHEAD 1, LETTERHEAD 2, LETTERHEAD 3 or LETTERHEAD 4, depending upon which one you are creating.

7. Choose **D**escription (3)

8. Type the description and press **Enter**

LETTERHEAD 1	Name/address centered
LETTERHEAD 2	Name/address with line
LETTERHEAD 3	Name/address with graphic
LETTERHEAD 4	Name centered, address in shaded box

9. Choose **C**odes (4)

10. Enter the codes (see following pages)

11. Press *Exit* (**F7**) three times

12. Choose **S**ave (6)

13. Type **LTRHEADS.STY** and press **Enter**

14. Press *Exit* (**F7**)

Customizing the Style

To create your own letterhead, type your own name and address (and company name) instead of the sample information. If you wish, you can include a telephone number.

Letterhead 3 includes a graphic. If you do not want the border around the graphic, the following should be done before entering any of the other codes.

1. Press *Graphics* (**Alt-F9**)
2. Choose **F**igure (1)
3. Choose **O**ptions (4)
4. Choose **B**order Style (1)
5. Choose **N**one (1) four times
6. Press *Exit* (**F7**)

Style Name: Letterhead 1

Description: Name/address centered

Codes:

1. Press *Format* (**Shift-F8**)
2. Choose **L**ine (1)
3. Choose **J**ustification (3)
4. Choose **C**enter (2)
5. Press *Exit* (**F7**)
6. Press *Font* (**Ctrl-F8**)
7. Choose **S**ize (1)
8. Choose **L**arge (5)
9. Press *Bold* (**F6**)
10. Type **Jane Martin** and press **Enter**
11. Type **1234 State Street** and press **Enter**
12. Type **Santa Cruz, NM 57111**
13. Press *Font* (**Ctrl-F8**)
14. Choose **N**ormal (3)

15. Press **Enter** four times
16. Press *Format* (**Shift-F8**)
17. Choose **L**ine (1)
18. Choose **J**ustification (3)
19. Choose **L**eft (1)
20. Press *Exit* (**F7**)

Jane Martin
1234 State Street
Santa Cruz, NM 57111

THE CODES FOR "LETTERHEAD 1" LOOK LIKE THIS:

[Just:Center][LARGE][BOLD]Jane Martin[HRt] 1234 State Street[HRt] Santa Cruz, NM 57111[bold][large][HRt] [HRt][HRt][HRt][Just:Left]

Style Name: Letterhead 2

Description: Name/address with line

Codes:

1. Press *Center* (**Shift-F6**)
2. Press *Bold* (**F6**)
3. Type **Jane Martin**
4. Press **Space Bar** five times
5. Type **1234 State Street**
6. Press **Space Bar** five times
7. Type **Santa Cruz, NM 57111**
8. Press *Bold* (**F6**)
9. Press **Enter**
10. Press *Graphics* (**Alt-F9**)
11. Choose **L**ine (5)
12. Choose **H**orizontal (1)
13. Choose **W**idth of Line (4)
14. Type **0.05** and press **Enter**
15. Press *Exit* (**F7**)
16. Press **Enter** twice

Jane Martin   1234 State Street   Santa Cruz, NM 57111

THE CODES FOR "LETTERHEAD 2" LOOK LIKE THIS:

[Center][BOLD]Jane Martin   1234 State Street   Santa
Cruz, NM 57111[bold][HRt][HLine:Full,Baseline,6.5",
0.05",100%][HRt][HRt][HRt]

Style Name: Letterhead 3

Description: Name/address with graphic

Codes:

1. Press *Graphics* (**Alt-F9**)
2. Choose **F**igure (1)
3. Choose **C**reate (1)
4. Choose **F**ilename (1)
5. Type **GLOBE2-M.WPG** and press **Enter**
6. Choose **S**ize (7)
7. Choose **H**eight (2)
8. Type **1** and press **Enter**
9. Press *Exit* (**F7**)
10. Press *Bold* (**F6**)
11. Press *Font* (**Ctrl-F8**)
12. Choose **S**ize (1)
13. Choose **V**ery Large (6)
14. Type **IMPORT-EXPORT SERVICES**
15. Press *Font* (**Ctrl-F8**)
16. Choose **S**ize (1)
17. Choose **V**ery Large (6)
18. Press **Enter**
19. Press **Tab** twice
20. Type **Jane Martin** and press **Enter**
21. Press **Tab** twice
22. Type **1234 State Street** and press **Enter**
23. Press **Tab** twice
24. Type **Santa Cruz, NM 57111**
25. Press *Bold* (**F6**)
26. Press **Enter** four times

IMPORT-EXPORT SERVICES

**Jane Martin
1234 State Street
Santa Cruz, NM 57111**

THE CODES FOR "LETTERHEAD 3" LOOK LIKE THIS:

[Fig Opt][Fig Box:1;MAP-WORL.WPG;][BOLD][VRY LARGE]IMPORT-EXPORT SERVICES[vry large][HRt][Tab][Tab]Jane Martin[HRt][Tab][Tab]1234 State Street[HRt][Tab][Tab]Santa Cruz, NM 57111[bold][HRt][HRt][HRt]

Style Name: Letterhead 4

Description: Name centered, address in shaded box

Codes:

1. Press *Center* (**Shift-F6**)
2. Press *Bold* (**F6**)
3. Press *Font* (**Ctrl-F8**)
4. Choose <u>S</u>ize (1)
5. Choose <u>E</u>xt Large (7)
6. Type **Jane Martin**
7. Press *Font* (**Ctrl-F8**)
8. Choose <u>N</u>ormal (3)
9. Press **Enter**
10. Press *Graphics* (**Alt-F9**)
11. Choose Text <u>B</u>ox (3)
12. Choose <u>O</u>ptions (4)
13. Choose <u>B</u>order Style (1)
14. Choose <u>T</u>hick (6) twice
15. Press **Enter** three times
16. Press *Graphics* (**Alt-F9**)
17. Choose Text <u>B</u>ox (3)
18. Choose <u>C</u>reate (1)
19. Choose <u>H</u>orizontal Position (6)
20. Choose <u>F</u>ull (4)
21. Choose <u>E</u>dit (9)
22. Press *Bold* (**F6**)
23. Type **1234 State Street**
24. Press *Flush Right* (**Alt-F6**)
25. Type **Santa Cruz, NM 57111**

26. Press *Bold* (**F6**)

27. Press *Exit* (**F7**) twice

28. Press **Enter** twice

Jane Martin

1234 State Street	**Santa Cruz, NM 57111**

THE CODES FOR "LETTERHEAD 4" LOOK LIKE THIS:

[Center][BOLD][EXT LARGE]Jane Martin[ext large][bold]
[HRt][Txt Opt][Text Box:1;;][HRt][HRt]

Suggestions for Other Styles

Newsletters

Because the preparation of newsletters involves repetitive formatting, styles are a great help. If you were going to publish a newsletter, it would be useful if you could work with the text in a draft format with monospaced  type. Although you will eventually want to have it in columns with font sizes and types that will look good on the final copy, it is much easier to work with the information in a monospaced draft form.

The trick is to have two style libraries that contain styles with duplicate names (see the following suggested styles). Choose DRAFT.STY when you want to work in a monospaced draft mode. When you want to see it in final form, retrieve FINAL.STY and answer Y (YES) to the following prompt from WordPerfect:

Style(s) already exist. Replace? No (Yes).

If you want to go back to seeing it in draft form, retrieve DRAFT.STY and tell WordPerfect to overwrite again. That way, you can see it in final form any time you want but you can work with it in a much more manageable form.

In summary, when you have two groups of styles with the same style names, you can change the formatting of a document as many times as you like by simply retrieving the other style library.

Suggested Style Library for Newsletters— FINAL.STY

Masthead (open style that sets up the overall format, font choices, headers, footers, column definition, column on, etc.)

Articles (paired style for each news item, perhaps with short graphic line to accent the subheading)

Suggested Style Library for Newsletters— DRAFT.STY

Masthead (open style with monospaced font, no columns)

Articles (paired style perhaps with only underlining)

Frequently Used Text

You can store frequently used paragraphs as separate open styles in a style library. Whenever you want to insert a particular paragraph, turn that style on.

Invoices

You can create an open style that contains the overall formatting and the heading for an invoice. This is useful to have in a separate style in order to be able to use the same style for a number of forms. Create a second open style to be used specifically for invoices. This style would contain the column headings, tab sets, math definition, and math on code.

Lesson 7 Summary

The following is a listing of the practice exercise styles. In addition to actual practices, suggestions are included covering newsletters, frequently used text, and invoices.

Type of Style	Name of Style	Description of Style
Paired Style	CHAPTER NUMBER	Chapter number with ToC marking
	CHAPTER TITLE	Chapter title with ToC marking
	ENVELOPE	9x4 envelope w/o ret. add.
	HANGING	Used for series of hanging paragraphs
	LIST	Used for bulleted list
	QUOTATION	Used for long quotations
	TITLE	Centered, bolded, very large
Outline Style	OUTLINE	Bold, indented
Open Style	LETTERHEAD 1	Name/address centered
	LETTERHEAD 2	Name/address with line
	LETTERHEAD 3	Name/address with graphic
	LETTERHEAD 4	Name centered, address in shaded box

Notes

Notes

_____

_____

_____

_____

_____

_____

_____

_____

_____

_____

_____

_____

_____

_____

_____

_____

_____

_____

_____

_____

_____

_____

_____

Index

Retrieving styles, 44, 63-65,
    86, 87, 96
Reveal codes, 35, 38, 42
Right par, 54

S

Saving styles, 49-56
Selecting styles
    open styles, 36
    outline styles, 43
    paired styles, 38
STY, 37, 40, 44, 53
Style Codes screen, 20, 25
Style definition, 1
Style Edit screen, 19, 21, 23,
    26, 28
Style library, 18, 22, 27, 35,
    37, 38, 40, 44, 49, 50,
    52, 53, 55, 60-65, 83,
    96, 97
Style List screen, 17, 18, 21,
    22, 26, 27, 30, 36, 39
Style name, 19, 23, 28
Style type examples, 11-13
STYLES subdirectory, 51

T

Tech init, 54
Technical, 54
Term paper, 11
Theses, 11, 14, 79
Title, 3, 24, 70, 71, 83, 86,
    87
Turning off paired styles, 41,
    73
Turning on paired styles, 39
Types of styles, 9-14

U

Updating styles, 65
Using styles, 35-46
    open styles, 35, 45
    outline styles, 42, 45
    paired styles, 38

W

WordPerfect 5.0, 5
WPS, 37, 40, 44, 53

About Crisp Publications

We hope that you enjoyed this book. If so, we have good news for you. This title is only one in the library of Crisp's best-selling books. Each of our books is easy to use and is obtainable at a very reasonable price.

Books are available from your distributor. A free catalog is available upon request from Crisp Publications, Inc., 1200 Hamilton Court, Menlo Park, California 94025. Phone: (800) 442-7477; Fax: (415) 323-5800.

Books are organized by general subject area.